Rebeca Andrade
The Heart of Brazilian Gymnastics- Overcoming the Odds

Benny M. Williams

Copyright

All rights reserved. No part of this publication may be reproduced, distributed, or transmitted in any form or by any means, including photocopying, recording, and other electronic or mechanical methods, without prior written permission of the publisher, except in case of briefs quotation embodied in critical reviews and certain other noncommercial uses permitted by copyright law.

Copyright © Benny M. Williams,2024

Table of content

Introduction

Chapter 1: Early Life and Background

Entry into Gymnastics

Chapter 2: Breakthrough in National Competitions

International Debut and Early Success

Chapter 3: Overcoming Injuries and Setbacks

2020 Tokyo Olympics Success

Major Championships and Achievements

Chapter 4: Signature Skills and Routines

Chapter 5: Training and Coaching Team

Chapter 6: Role Model and Influence in Brazilian Sports

Personal Life and Interests

Chapter 7: Legacy and Impact on Gymnastics

Conclusion

Introduction

Athlete Rebeca Andrade has become one of the most famous names in gymnastics thanks to her amazing skills, strength, and unwavering drive. Rebeca was born on May 8, 1999, in Guarulhos, Brazil. It wasn't easy for her to become famous around the world. Growing up in a big family with little money meant that Rebeca had to deal with a lot of problems that would have stopped many people from following their dreams. However, it was these problems that made her who she is and drove her desire to do well.

From a very young age, Rebeca had an obvious love for gymnastics. The teachers at a nearby gymnastics school saw her natural speed, strength, and grace and quickly realized how talented she was. But getting to the top of professional gymnastics is often a hard road, and Rebeca's was no different. She had trouble getting to the best training facilities, tools, and coaches because she didn't have enough money, but her family and community rallied behind her and were determined to help her reach her goals in any way they could.

As Rebeca's skills improved, so did the things she had to give up to reach her goals. Her new life consisted of spending a lot of time in the gym, following strict workout plans, and always feeling like she had to perform at her best. Even with these problems, Rebeca didn't lose sight of her goals. She was always trying to get better and promote her country on the world stage. She quickly rose through the ranks of Brazilian gymnastics, and she quickly became one of the best prospects in the country, fighting against older athletes at a young age.

But Rebeca's rise to fame was hampered by mishaps, especially injuries that seemed likely to end her career. Her mental and physical strength was put to the test by several serious injuries, including multiple knee surgeries. She tore her anterior cruciate ligament (ACL), which is the most serious of these injuries and can often end an athlete's career. Rebeca's recovery was very hard. It took her months of therapy and hard work to get her strength and movement back. Many athletes would have given up after these failures, but Rebeca refused to let them define her. Rather than giving up, she used these tough times to get stronger, both mentally and physically.

She worked hard and made an amazing return at the 2020 Tokyo Olympics, where she made history. Rebeca won a gold medal in the vault and a silver medal in the all-around competition after years of hard work and what seemed like impossible challenges. This was a huge accomplishment because she was the first Brazilian gymnast to ever win an Olympic gold medal. This was a big deal not only in Brazil but also in the gymnastics community around the world. In a sport that had mostly been dominated by athletes from the US, Russia, and China, her win was more than just an individual success; it was a turning point for Brazilian gymnastics.

Fans all over the world were amazed and impressed by Rebeca's show in Tokyo. Her routines were the perfect mix of strength, accuracy, and artistry, showing off her amazing skills on a variety of platforms. But more than her mechanical skills, what struck people was her story of persistence. She became an example and source of hope for athletes all over the world, especially those from poor families who, like Rebeca, face challenges while trying to follow their dreams.

The sport in Brazil has also changed a lot because of her success. As a leader, Rebeca has made it possible for other Brazilian gymnasts to follow in her footsteps. She has shown that athletes from countries that don't have as many resources as traditional gymnastics powerhouses can still reach the top of the sport if they work hard, don't give up, and get help. She has a bigger impact than just getting medals; she still motivates young athletes to dream big and work hard to reach their targets.

Rebeca Andrade's story is one of victory over hardship, and it shows how she never gave up on doing her best, no matter what. Millions of people love her story of how she went from being a little girl in Guarulhos to becoming an Olympic winner. She is remembered as one of the best gymnasts of her time. She has changed what is possible for gymnasts from countries that don't have many of them, and she is now a role model for gymnasts all over the world, not just in Brazil.

Her accomplishments show how important it is to keep going even when things get hard and to always believe in your abilities. As Rebeca Andrade continues to push the limits of her sport, she leaves a legacy that encourages others to do the same and shows that no dream or task is too big. There is no question that Rebeca Andrade's story is far from over as she looks to the future. She has more competition and goals in mind. Her story keeps inspiring and motivating people, and it will always be remembered in the world of gymnastics.

Chapter 1: Early Life and Background

She was born in Guarulhos, a city in the state of São Paulo, Brazil, on May 8, 1999. Living in a big family with seven brothers meant that she had to deal with the problems that come with having a lot of them. Even with all of these problems, Rebeca's family has always been there for her. Rosa, her mother, worked hard to take care of her kids, and Rebeca's gymnastics skills were clear from a young age.

Even though Rebeca lived in a simple house, she found happiness and freedom in being active. She loved to move around even when she was a little girl, flipping and sliding wherever she could. When Rebeca was four years old, her mother saw that her daughter was naturally good at gymnastics and signed her up for a local gym. Even though it meant making a lot of sacrifices, this choice would set the course for Rebeca's future. Her family didn't have the money to pay for top-level training, but Rebeca's skills started to grow with the help of her mother and coaches who saw her promise.

Even though she didn't have a lot of money or other means, Rebeca was always dedicated to gymnastics. At her neighbourhood gym, she quickly became one of the best, which caught the attention of coaches at a higher level. Her unique mix of strength, grace, and athleticism made her stand out from her friends, and she wasn't asked to join a more competitive gymnastics school for long.

It wasn't easy to get to the top of gymnastics when you grew up in a working-class home. The cost of travel, training, and tools made things even harder than they were before. But Rebeca was determined, and her family was always there for her. This helped her move forward. She knew even as a child that people were giving up things so she could follow her dreams, and she was determined to seize every chance that came her way.

As Rebeca got better at gymnastics, she had to deal with the problems that come with the sport, like strict training plans, long hours in the gym, and the stress and strain of competition. She stayed focused on her goals through it all. Her teachers often said how strong she was and how she could deal with problems, even though she was young. Because Rebeca loved gymnastics so much, she worked harder and always tried to get better.

The people in her neighbourhood also had a big impact on her growth. The people in her community were proud of her success, and many came together to help her in any way they could. Many people helped Rebeca get to the top of her game. Her family, teachers, and community all worked hard.

The early years and history of Rebeca shaped her into the champion she would become. She learned to be tough, determined, and grateful for every chance she got by growing up in a family that loved her but didn't have a lot of money. She had these traits that would help her get through the tough parts of her job, like the long, hard workouts and injuries that almost put her plans on hold. Rebeca never forgot how much gymnastics made her happy or how much she wanted to serve her country on the world stage.

Entry into Gymnastics

When Rebeca Andrade first started gymnastics, it was almost by accident. But it quickly became her life's love. Even though she was born into a poor family, she had all the energy and curiosity that normal young children have. Rosa, Rebeca's mother, quickly noticed that her daughter was very good at physical activities. She was always spinning, running, and playing in ways that made her stand out from her friends. Rosa decided to sign her daughter Rebeca up for a local gymnastics program when she was four years old. This move would change her daughter's life forever.

As part of a government-funded program, Rebeca joined a program that gave kids from low-income families access to sports. Even though there weren't many tools, it was Rebeca's first experience with gymnastics and a chance to see what she could do. From the moment she walked into the gym, it was clear that she was meant to be there. Her teachers saw right away that she was naturally good at gymnastics and loved the difficult routines and moves. She was very good at simple skills, even though she was young, and her eagerness to learn was clear in every practice.

Rebeca loved the gym so much that it was like a second home to her. She quickly became more dedicated to gymnastics than many of her friends. She worked so hard that she often stayed late to practice and was always trying to get better. Her early coaches said she was a happy, focused athlete who was always ready to take on new tasks. She was great at gymnastics because it was competitive and required her to be precise, strong, and flexible.

Rebeca's chances to fight and train at a higher level started to open up as her skills became more clear. Her coaches looked for more advanced training options for her, even though it was hard for her family to pay for her to go. Money problems were always a problem because professional gymnastics needed a lot of money for things like travel, equipment, and more specialised coaching. Still, Rebeca was talented, and everyone around her did everything they could to help her keep getting better.

These problems were solved by Rebeca's determination, her mother's help, and the people in her neighbourhood. The drive of her family and the support of people who saw her promise kept her going even when they couldn't afford the gear or travel costs for competitions. She was certainly dedicated, which made it clear that she was ready to do anything to succeed in the sport.

By the time she was nine, Rebeca had already made a name for herself in area competitions. Her strength and grace made her stand out, and these qualities would later define her performances on the world stage. Because she did well in these early competitions, she was able to join a more advanced gymnastics school that could give her the training she needed to become a world-class athlete. For Rebeca, this change was a big turning point because it meant leaving her neighbourhood gym and going to a place that would push her to new heights.

In her first few years of gymnastics, Rebeca grew very quickly as she learned more difficult skills and routines. Her coaches were impressed by how well she handled the stress of competition at such a young age. She was regularly one of the best gymnasts in Brazil for her age group. There were costs that went along with this success, though. Rebeca spent a lot of time in the gym. She often had to balance schoolwork with a tough training plan, and she had to deal with the stress of competing as a young person.

Even though things were hard, her love for the sport never changed. As a creative outlet, gymnastics gave her a way to express herself physically, which she couldn't do outside of the gym. It was clear that Rebeca loved gymnastics and that it had become an important part of who she was.

Her first day of gymnastics was the start of an amazing journey that would be full of both victories and challenges. Through a program funded by the government, Rebeca worked her way up through the ranks of Brazilian gymnastics. Her early years in the sport paved the way for her to become a great athlete. In the years that followed, her big break on the world stage was made possible by her love of gymnastics, her hard work, and the unwavering support of her family.

Chapter 2:Breakthrough in National Competitions

When Rebeca Andrade made it to the national competitions, it was a big moment in her gymnastics career. She went from being a bright young talent to a rising star in Brazil. She trained hard for years, dealt with money problems, and learned how to handle the challenges of youth competitions. As she moved up in national tournaments, her hard work and natural skill started to pay off.

We saw her first big breakthrough at the Brazilian National Championships, where her strong skills caught the eye of both gymnastics fans and officials. Rebeca was already a star when she was in her early teens. She competed against dancers with more experience and often did better than them. Especially on the vault and floor, her routines showed off her raw strength, accuracy, and rare ease for someone her age. These things made her a tough rival, and the fact that she could consistently do difficult routines helped her stand out.

Rebeca proved herself to be one of the best gymnasts in Brazil at the 2012 National Championships. Amazingly, she won her first national title in the all-around event at just 13 years old, given how old she was and how tough the competition was. This win made it clear that she was going to be very successful. Her strong results on all four apparatuses—the vault, the uneven bars, the beam, and the floor exercise—showed how versatile she was as a gymnast. This would become one of her trademarks as she got older.

After this win, Rebeca's name became linked to excellence in Brazilian gymnastics. As it became clearer that she could fight on a global level, she quickly became the favourite to represent Brazil in international events. She continued to be the best at national competitions by always finishing in the top three and often getting gold in the all-around and individual apparatus finals.

One thing that made Rebeca's gymnastics stand out was that she could do well when she was under a lot of stress. A lot of young players have trouble with the mental demands of competition, but Rebeca seemed to do well in these situations. She kept her cool and focused during important events, which let her give her best performances when they meant the most. This mental toughness was especially important in national competitions, where there was a lot of pressure to do well in front of home fans and people who chose foreign teams.

Even though Rebeca was getting more and more successful, her path wasn't always easy. At this point in her career, she started to get hurt a lot, mostly to her knee. These injuries always got in the way of her growth, but they also showed how strong she was. She was determined to come back stronger and more focused even when she had failures that kept her out of action for months at a time. She became known as one of Brazil's toughest athletes after being hurt and then being able to recover and keep fighting at a high level.

As Rebeca continued to do well in national events, she started getting chances to compete anywhere in the world. Officials and coaches in Brazilian gymnastics saw that she had what it took to fight on the world stage, and she was soon chosen to represent Brazil in several international events. Her big break on the national stage not only showed how talented she was but also hinted at what was to come in her growing career abroad.

The fact that Rebeca did well in national events also helped gymnastics become more popular in Brazil. She was a young, charming athlete with obvious skill. Young people all over the country looked up to her as a gymnast. It was especially inspiring for young players from poor families to see how she overcame personal and financial problems to become the best in her sport. Gymnastics wasn't a popular sport in Rebeca's home country before she won national competitions. This raised the sport's standing and inspired a new generation of gymnasts.

Her many wins at national championships helped her get to even bigger and better things in foreign competitions. It was only a matter of time before Rebeca Andrade made her mark on the world stage. She was rapidly becoming the face of Brazilian gymnastics. These early wins set the stage for Rebeca's great accomplishments in the years to come. Soon, her name would be known not only in Brazil but all over the world.

International Debut and Early Success

Rebeca Andrade's international debut and early success paved the way for her to become known as one of the best gymnasts of her age around the world. After winning all of Brazil's national events, it was only a matter of time before Rebeca's skills were seen around the world. When she first competed in international events, it showed how good she was and how well she could do against the best gymnasts in the world. This made her a dangerous gymnast.

The first time Rebeca competed internationally was at the South American Gymnastics Championships in Chile in 2012. She made a big impact right away. She won many trophies, including gold in the all-around category, even though she was only 13 years old. She showed her signature mix of power, grace, and technical skill in this performance, which was an early sign that she would be able to do well against foreign competition. Her success in Chile made her one of Brazil's biggest young stars and paved the way for her future in the sport.

After her success in South America, Rebeca started to compete in bigger foreign events, where she continued to make a name for herself. She made one of her first big foreign shows at the Gymnix Foreign in Montreal, Canada, in 2013. Rebeca competed against some of the best gymnasts in the world. Her routines, especially on the vault and floor exercise, made her stand out, and she won a gold award in the vault, making her even more of a rising star in the sport.

As Rebeca's business grew internationally, she continued to compete in different events in 2013 and 2014, always coming in first or second place. But Rebeca shone at the Junior Pan American Championships in 2014. She won five gold medals, including the all-around title, while competing for Brazil's youth national team. She also won gold on the vault, uneven bars, balance beam, and floor exercise. Everything about her performances was amazing. She did better than her competitors in every event, showing how versatile she is as a gymnast.

Her huge success at the Junior Pan American Championships cemented her place as one of the best junior gymnasts in the world and brought her a lot of attention in the gymnastics world. It was clear from Rebeca's win that she was a serious contender for future senior-level competitions, which helped raise the profile of Brazilian gymnastics on the world stage. People all over the world became interested in gymnastics after she won gold medals. They started to see her as one of the sport's most potential young athletes.

It wasn't always easy for Rebeca to do well in her early foreign competitions. When she moved up to senior-level events, it was harder for her to keep up her high level of performance because she was up against gymnasts with more experience. Rebeca had to deal with the stress of competing internationally as well as illnesses that were starting to hurt her career. The fact that she kept going even after these failures shows what an amazing athlete she is for being so young.

By 2015, Rebeca had competed as a senior for the first time at the World Artistic Gymnastics Championships in Glasgow, Scotland. She did well for someone who was only 16 years old at the time, especially on vault, where she made it to the final and came in eighth. Her performance against the best gymnasts in the world showed that she had what it takes to compete at the top level of the sport, even though she didn't win a medal. The World Championships were a big moment in her career because they were her first big challenge at the senior level. They also marked the start of a long and successful international career.

Early success in other countries for Rebbeca set the stage for a career that would change the world. She consistently won junior and senior-level events, showing that she was not only a rising star in Brazilian gymnastics but also a serious contender in the global gymnastics community. Her performances against top competitors showed that she could do well on the world stage. Her early wins showed how talented, hardworking, and tough she was as she faced the difficulties of going from being a national star to an international one.

The years she spent competing internationally helped her build the skills that would help her do amazing things in the future, like her great performances at the Olympics and World Championships. Early success on the international stage for Rebeca Andrade showed that she had the skills and drive to become one of the best gymnasts in the world. But she was just getting started on her journey.

Chapter 3:Overcoming Injuries and Setbacks

For Rebeca Andrade, her work has been full of both amazing accomplishments and big problems, especially the injuries and setbacks she has had to deal with. These problems have put her strength and dedication to the sport to the test by showing how strong and determined she is.

Rebeca's career started to suffer from injuries around 2015, not long after she moved up to senior-level gymnastics. The sport's tough physical requirements and the stress of high-level competition were too much for her body. One of the biggest hurdles was when Rebeca hurt her knee badly at the beginning of 2016. She tore her anterior cruciate ligament (ACL), which is a common but serious injury for sports that usually needs a lot of surgery and recovery time. Not only did the torn ACL keep her out for months, but it also made people question her ability to get back to her old self.

The path to healing was long and hard. ACL rehabilitation includes both surgery to fix the tear and a strict physical treatment program to get the knee stronger, more flexible, and able to do its job again. Rebbeca had a hard time getting better, both physically and mentally. Being away from other competitors and being frustrated at not being able to do her best pushed her to her limits. Rebeca, on the other hand, attacked her recovery with the same drive that had made her famous up to that point. To get her power and confidence back, she worked closely with her medical team and stuck to a strict plan.

Even though Rebeca made some progress in her healing, she ran into more problems. There was another injury in 2017; this time it was to her shoulder. The injury meant she had to have more surgery and recovery time, which made her return to competition gymnastics even later than planned. She was hurt a lot and had to take time away from sports, which made her unsure about her future. With each failure, she had to rethink her plans and goals and deal with the emotional effects of being pushed to the sidelines.

Being able to get through these problems showed how strong and characterful Rebeca was. During the times she was healing, she kept a good attitude and helped her teammates, even though she couldn't participate herself. Her mental health was just as important as her physical health because she had to stay focused and determined no matter what.

Her hard work paid off, and she did well when she went back to competing. The best part of Rebeca's comeback was her success at the 2018 World Artistic Gymnastics Championships in Doha, Qatar.

She had a great performance, especially on vault, where she placed fifth, even though she had been having trouble. This performance showed that she could deal with problems and still perform at a high level.

When Rebeca participated in the Tokyo Olympics in 2020, it was the culmination of all her hard work. She had been hurt for years, but her show in Tokyo was nothing less than amazing. She was the first Brazilian gymnast to win an Olympic gold medal. She won a gold medal in the vault and a silver medal in the all-around. This accomplishment showed how strong she was and was the result of years of hard work and healing.

Rebeca Andrade's story of injuries and failures shows how hard it is for professional athletes. Even with these problems, she was able to get back to her best performance, which shows how strong she is both physically and mentally. Even though each failure was scary, they all helped her become a better athlete and be successful on the world stage.

Many people find inspiration in her story, which shows that with hard work, persistence, and a good attitude, you can get through anything. Because of how well she did after getting hurt, Rebeca became one of the best gymnasts in the world and a symbol of power and resilience. She is an inspiration to aspiring athletes everywhere because she overcame hardship and achieved her goals. She shows that the road to success is often paved with challenges, but it is overcoming these challenges that truly defines greatness.

2020 Tokyo Olympics Success

Rebeca Andrade's success at the 2020 Olympics in Tokyo is one of the most impressive things she has ever done in gymnastics and the history of Brazilian sports. Due to the COVID-19 pandemic, the Tokyo Games had to be pushed back to 2021. It was there that Andrade made history by becoming one of the best athletes at the game.

Before she went to the Olympics, Rebeca had already been through a lot. On her way to Tokyo, she had a lot of injuries and setbacks that showed how strong and determined she was. But all of her hard work and time spent training paid off with a performance that changed her career and had a big effect on the sport.

In Tokyo, Rebeca's journey started with the qualification round, where she showed off her amazing skills and calmness. She did great on all of the equipment, but especially on the vault and the floor exercise. In both the all-around and vault events, she made it to the finals, which set the stage for what would be a great battle for her.

The gymnastics world was blown away by Rebeca's performance in the all-around final on July 29, 2021. She did her routines with a mix of strong tumbling, exact execution, and beautiful artistry. There were some of the best gymnasts in the world competing against her, including the pick, Simone Biles of the United States. All four of Rebeca's performances—the vault, the uneven bars, the balance beam, and the floor exercise—were perfect and very tough to do.

With her performance, Rebeca got a score that won her the silver medal in the all-around competition. This was a big deal because it was the first time a Brazilian gymnast won an Olympic medal in the all-around event. Her silver medal showed how much she had worked, how skilled she was, and how dedicated she had been to her job. It was a proud moment for Brazil and a clear sign that she was one of the best gymnasts in the world.

The most exciting part of Rebeca's Olympic trip was the vault final on August 1, 2021. She did two great vaults at this event, showing off her strong launch and excellent execution. During her routines, she did a Cheng and a handspring double front, which were both very precise and hard to do. She got a high score for her vaults because of how high, well-formed, and safely they landed. This helped her win the gold title.

The gold medal that Rebeca Andrade won in the vault was a memorable moment. She was the first gymnast from Brazil to win an Olympic gold medal, which had not been done by any other gymnasts in the country before. Her win not only made her a better gymnast, but it also brought Brazilian gymnastics to the world's attention in a way that had never been seen before.

Her success in Tokyo was praised in Brazil and around the world. People praised Rebeca's acts for being technically perfect and having a lot of emotional depth. She was also able to perform well under pressure, which showed how mentally strong and focused she was. The praise she got showed how much she had worked hard, made sacrifices, and been strong throughout her career.

The things Rebeca did at the 2020 Olympics in Tokyo also had a big effect on the sport in Brazil. Her success motivated a new generation of gymnasts and gave the sport more attention and support across the country. Given the historical value of her gold medal in the vault and silver medal in the all-around, she became a legend in Brazilian sports history.

Rebeca Andrade's career took a big turn at the Tokyo Olympics. Her performances not only made her one of the best dancers in the world, but they also showed that she could deal with problems and still do great things. Her success at the Olympics came after years of hard work, persistence, and dedication. It cemented her place as one of the most famous gymnastics athletes of all time.

Major Championships and Achievements

For Rebeca Andrade, her career in gymnastics is marked by a string of impressive wins at big championships that show how talented and tough she is. In addition to the Olympics, she has done well at the World Championships, the Pan American Games, and other international events. All of these have helped her become one of the best gymnasts of her age.

At the 2013 Gymnix International in Montreal, Canada, Rebeca did one of her first big things. It was one of her first big foreign events, so it was a big deal for her career. She showed how good she was on vault and floor exercise by winning gold awards at Gymnix International. This set her up for future success. Her performances were known for their power and accuracy, which made her famous on the gymnastics tour around the world.

At the 2014 Junior Pan American Championships, Rebeca continued to do very well and put on a great show. She won five gold medals, in the floor exercise, uneven bars, all-around, vault, and uneven bars. This incredible accomplishment showed how skilled and versatile she was on all platforms. It made her the most popular gymnast in junior gymnastics and got a lot of attention from gymnasts around the world.

At the 2015 World Artistic Gymnastics Championships in Glasgow, Scotland, Rebeca competed for the first time at the senior level. She placed eighth in the vault final, going up against some of the best gymnasts in the world. This showed that she could fight at a high level even though she was new to senior competition. This victory was a big deal, and it showed that she could do well in the sport in the future.

In 2016, Rebeca Andrade's career was temporarily put on hold when she hurt her knee badly enough that she needed surgery and a lot of time to heal. Even though this setback happened, she made an amazing recovery. The best thing about her comeback was how she did at the 2017 World Artistic Gymnastics Championships in Montreal, Canada. Even though she had to deal with extra problems because she had recently hurt herself, Rebeca performed well and made it to the vault final, where she finished in fifth place. The way she performed showed how strong and determined she was.

At the 2018 World Artistic Gymnastics Championships in Doha, Qatar, Rebeca did some amazing things. She was very good at the competition, especially on vault, where she came in fifth place. Her performances in Doha showed that she is still one of the best gymnasts in the world and that she can fight with them.

Another big event in Rebeca's journey was the 2019 Pan American Games in Lima, Peru. Four gold medals were hers for her amazing effort in the all-around, vault, uneven bars, and floor exercise. Her performance at these games showed how good she is at the sport and confirmed that she is one of the best gymnasts in the Americas.

The 2020 Tokyo Olympics, which were moved to 2021 because of the COVID-19 outbreak, were a turning point for Rebeca Andrade. She got a gold medal in the vault and a silver medal in the all-around event at the Olympics. She made history when she won the vault by being the first Brazilian gymnast to ever win an Olympic gold medal. It was also a historic win for her because it was the first time in Olympic history that a Brazilian dancer won a medal in the all-around event.

Rebeca continued to do well at foreign events after her success at the Olympics. At the 2021 World Artistic Gymnastics Championships in Kitakyushu, Japan, she continued to compete at a high level and solidified her place as one of the best gymnasts in the world.

The important titles and accomplishments that Rebeca Andrade has earned show how talented, hardworking, and tough she is. She is one of the best gymnasts of her time because of how well she has done in international competitions. She has also helped make Brazilian gymnastics famous around the world. All of these accomplishments show how skilled, dedicated, and able she was to do well in big events, cementing her place as a famous person in the sport.

Chapter 4: Signature Skills and Routines

Rebeca Andrade's signature skills and routines have become the defining features of her career, showing off her exceptional technical skill, artistic flair, and quick performance across a wide range of instruments. Many people love her acts because they are both hard and interesting for both the audience and the judges. Each piece of equipment shows a different aspect of her gymnastics skills. Together, they show the power, accuracy, and creativity that have made her career famous.

On the vault, Rebeca's moves are known for how hard they are and how well they are done. The Cheng, which is a front handspring with a full twist, is her signature vault. This vault is very hard because you have to move quickly and precisely to do the twist and stay in control during the fall.

Rebeca does the Cheng with amazing height and control, showing off her explosive strength and precise skill. The vault is notoriously hard, and Rebeca's skill at doing difficult moves under pressure is a true testament to her skill. The handspring double front is another impressive jump she can do. This move starts with a handspring and then goes through two flips in the air before landing. The handspring double front is one of the hardest jumps in gymnastics because you have to be very careful to land safely after doing several flips. Rebecca's strength and control show in how well she does this vault, as well as her ability to land the move cleanly and with control.

When Rebeca does the floor exercise, her routines stand out because they have strong tumbling moves and fun choreography. A lot of the time, her floor performances include a bunch of dynamic tumbling passes, like the Arabian double pike and the double layout. The Arabian double pike has a half-twist and two flips in a pike position, while the double layout has two flips from a high-flying layout position. For both passes, you need to be very strong and fast and time your moves perfectly. Rebeca's athleticism and technical skill are shown by how well she can do these moves with power and ease. Rebeca is known for both her tumbling passes and the expressive choreography and performance quality of her floor acts. A lot of the time, her routines include dance and expressive movements that go well with her tumbling and make the whole show better. Because she is both athletic and artistic, her dance routines are both technically impressive and emotionally thrilling.

Rebeca's moves on the balance beam show how well she can balance, be precise, and look beautiful. The balance beam is hard to use because it's not very wide and you have to be very accurate when doing acrobatics on it. There are a lot of tough moves in

Rebeca's beam routines, like aerials, back handsprings, and complicated dismounts. For each of these things, you need to be physically strong and have great balance and rhythm. Rebeca's technical skill and control are shown by how well she can do these elements with little wobbling and a smooth flow of moves. Her beam routines are also very beautiful, with smooth changes between moves. This shows that she can combine technical skills with artistic expression.

Rebeca is also very good on the uneven bars, where she shows off her strength and balance by combining release moves and transitions in very complex ways. The Jaeger, a release move that includes catching and re-grasping the bar while flying, is one of her signature moves on the bars. To use the Jaeger skill correctly, you need to be strong and time your moves perfectly. Rebeca's technical skill on the apparatus is shown by how well she can do this move with a clean catch and smooth transfer. Her bar routines also have a lot of tricky changes from one thing to another, which shows how coordinated and smooth she is. Rebeca's performances on the uneven bars are both very hard and very smooth, which shows how well she knows how to use the equipment after a lot of practice.

Rebeca Andrade's unique routines show how talented she is and how much she loves gymnastics. From the explosive power of her vaults to the graceful accuracy of her beam routines, each apparatus shows off a different part of her skills. She has won awards and recognition at major international competitions for her ability to blend technical difficulty with artistic expression. People love Rebeca's performances because they are well-executed, have interesting routines, and show that she can perform well under pressure at important events. Her routines not only show how good she is at gymnastics, but they also help build her image as one of the best gymnasts in the world.

Chapter 5:Training and Coaching Team

Reneca Andrade's rise to fame in gymnastics is a tribute to both her amazing skill and unwavering drive, as well as the unwavering support she receives from her training and coaching team. This team has been very important to her success and has helped her reach her full potential while dealing with the tough demands of top competition.

Rebeca's journey started at a gym in Brazil, where she learned about gymnastics for the first time. Early on, her teachers saw how talented she was and set the stage for her growth. These early years were very important for building her basic skills and knowledge of the sport. Rebeca's training became more organized as she went along, with a focus on improving her physical skills and routines for competitions.

It was a big change for Rebeca when she joined the São Caetano do Sul gym in 2015. It was a turning point in her career. The grounds and coaches at São Caetano do Sul are known to be among the best in the world. It was in this setting that Rebeca could learn more advanced training methods and compete at a higher level. She chose to move to this well-known gym because she wanted to get better and fight on an international level.

Rebeca started working with a group of skilled coaches at São Caetano do Sul. They were very important to her growth. Her head teacher was an important part of her training and gave her expert advice on all parts of gymnastics. This coach's job included more than just teaching techniques. They also had to help with planning strategies and giving mental support. The head coach's knowledge and experience were very helpful in planning

Rebeca's routines, coming up with her plans for competition, and helping her deal with the stress of high-level competition.

At São Caetano do Sul, the training schedule was strict and carefully planned. Every day, Rebeca did a mix of routines on apparatus, conditioning, and practising choreography. The severity of the workouts was meant to push her to her limits while still keeping an eye on her health and avoiding injuries. The sessions were designed to help her get better in specific areas, like improving her floor routines and perfecting her vault technique. Planning her training around making sure she did her best and was ready for foreign events was important.

Rebeca worked with more than just her head coach. She also had specialized teachers who worked with different equipment. For example, she had specific vault coaches who helped her with all of her vaulting moves, even the more difficult ones like the Cheng and the handspring double front. Specialized teachers helped her improve her routines on the uneven bars and the balance beam so she could perform with grace and accuracy. Each teacher brought a lot of knowledge and experience to the table and knew how to use their tools, which helped Rebeca do well overall.

Rebeca's training also included a lot of work with sports scientists and performance monitors. These experts kept an eye on her progress and evaluated her work using cutting-edge technology and data analysis. Motion analysis and biomechanical tests gave her more information about her technique, which helped her find ways to improve and keep track of her growth. By using science methods in Rebeca's training, her team could make decisions based on data that improved her performance and lowered her risk of getting hurt.

Physiotherapists, sports doctors, and other medical workers were very important to Rebeca's health and recovery. Because gymnastics is very hard on the body, it was important to avoid injuries and stay fit generally. Rebeca's medical team took care of her preventative needs, helped her recover from accidents, and made sure she stayed in top physical shape. Their help was especially important while she was healing from injuries, as it helped her deal with the hurdles of getting back to competitive form.

Rebeca's family, friends, and teachers were also very important to her success because they helped her feel better and kept her going. Their support helped her stay focused and strong, especially when things were hard, like when she was hurt or had to deal with the stress of high-stakes events. Her mental strength and overall health were helped by the good effects of her support network.

From her early days in local gyms to her success on the world stage, Rebeca Andrade's training and coaching team has been a big part of her success. The trainers, sports scientists, doctors, and people in her support network have all worked together to make a system that has helped her do well in the sport. Their knowledge, hard work, and support have been very important in helping Rebeca get through tough times, do amazing things, and become one of the best athletes in the world.

Chapter 6: Role Model and Influence in Brazilian Sports

In addition to her amazing gymnastics skills, Rebeca Andrade is a role model and has had a big impact on Brazilian sports. Her rise from a young gymnast-to-be to an Olympic winner has had a huge effect on Brazilian sports culture, inspiring many people and changing the way Brazilian athletes compete.

Rebeca's rise to fame shows how strong and determined she is, traits that many people relate to deeply. Her ability to get through tough situations, like being seriously hurt and having to deal with the stress of foreign competition, shows how important it is to keep going and work hard. The fact that she overcame all the changes in her story shows that success is possible even when things don't go as planned. This story has become an inspiration for young players who see Rebeca as someone who has been through tough times and come out on top through sheer determination and hard work.

Brazilian gymnastics has changed a lot because of her amazing performances at the 2020 Tokyo Olympics, where she won a gold medal in the vault and a silver medal in the all-around event. Not only did these achievements make history by giving Brazil its first Olympic gold medal in gymnastics, but they also made the sport more popular across the country than ever before. Rebeca's success has changed how people in Brazil think about gymnastics by showing that it is a sport that requires a lot of skill, focus, and athleticism. Because of this, gymnastics has gained more respect and attention from both the public and the sports community.

Rebeca's success can be seen most clearly in the fact that more and more young Brazilians are interested in and participating in gymnastics. A new breed of gymnasts is motivated by her success, which has led to a noticeable rise in the number of people joining gymnastics clubs and training programs across the country. Young athletes are more inspired to do gymnastics now that they see Rebeca's success. They want to reach their own athletic goals just like she did. This rise in interest shows how Rebeca has helped get more people interested in the sport and created a supportive setting for young athletes.

Rebeca has an impact on more than just gymnastics. She has an impact on all Brazilian sports. Gymnastics hasn't always been as important in Brazilian sports culture as football or volleyball. But Rebeca's accomplishments have made the sport much more well-known, which has raised its standing and importance. She has gotten more attention from the public, sports groups, and the media because of her success. This has helped people understand how hard it is to compete at the highest level.

Her effect also shows how important it is to keep investing in the growth and support of athletes. Rebeca's success has shown how important it is to give young players access to good training facilities, experienced coaches, and full support systems. Because of all the attention her accomplishments have gotten, there are now talks about improving the resources and facilities for sports programs all over Brazil to better help new talent grow. This focus on giving players better support shows how Rebeca is working to make the sports community a better place.

Rebeca has made a lot of important contributions to gymnastics and sports culture. She is also a well-known public figure who promotes good sportsmanship and success. Her work to improve the community, make public appearances, and speak out for others has made her even more of a positive impact. Rebeca keeps encouraging people to follow their dreams and make a difference through sports by talking about her own experiences and spreading the ideals of discipline, persistence, and hard work.

The role model Rebeca Andrade left behind and the impact she had on Brazilian sports are both deep and wide-reaching. Her accomplishments have made gymnastics a popular sport in Brazil, motivated a new generation of athletes, and sparked conversations about how to better help young athletes. Rebeca's hard work, resilience, and success have made her a symbol of what is possible with dedication and determination. She will leave a lasting mark on the world of sports and encourage future generations to aim for greatness.

Personal Life and Interests

The things that Rebeca Andrade likes to do in her free time show a lot about who she is outside of gymnastics. You can learn about her personality and the things that make her tick as an athlete and as a person by looking at her experiences, interests, and personal beliefs.

Rebecca Andrade was born in São Paulo, Brazil, on May 8, 1999. She grew up in a loving family that has been very important to her growth as a gymnast. Throughout her work, her family has always been there to cheer her on and help her. They have been a part of her journey from the beginning of her training to her success on the world stage. The strong bond with her family has been a big part of her strength and drive.

Rebeca was born and raised in São Paulo. She was very dedicated to gymnastics as a child. She became passionate about the sport at a young age, and her family's support made it possible for her to follow her dream. Rebeca was able to focus on her training and competition goals because her family was close and offered a stable and caring environment.

Rebeca has many interests and hobbies besides gymnastics that make her happy and healthy. Her love of music has been made clear, and she often turns to it to unwind. Music is a big part of her life; it helps her relax and it changes the way she does things every day. It helps her connect with the artistic and emotional parts of her shows and gives her routines more ways to express herself.

Also, Rebeca is really into fashion and has become very interested in style and design.

The fact that she likes fashion shows in the places she goes and the things she posts on social media, where she often shows off her style. Being creative and expressing herself through fashion is a way for her to do so outside of her athletic job.

Rebeca has been active in several community and charitable activities in addition to her interests. Giving back and supporting causes that matter to her is what she does with her fame. Her work with charities shows that she wants to make a difference in people's lives and use her wealth to help the community as a whole. As part of her charity work, Rebeca takes part in events and programs that help young people grow and learn about sports.

Rebeca wants to keep a balance between her busy gymnastics job and her personal life. She values time with family and friends because it helps her feel grounded and gives her a bigger picture. Her close friendships and social interactions are important for her mental health and provide a support system that goes well with her work successes.

Rebeca is a well-rounded person who values family, personal growth, and giving back to the community, as shown by her daily life and interests. In addition to gymnastics, she loves music, fashion, and doing good things for other people. Her strong family support and social ties help her succeed. Rebeca Andrade's ability to balance her work and home life shows how complex she is and how many sides she has.

Chapter 7:Legacy and Impact on Gymnastics

Many things about Rebeca Andrade have changed the sport of gymnastics, making her a truly important person in its history. Her efforts go beyond her accomplishments; they have affected the growth of gymnastics in Brazil and around the world.

The amazing things Rebeca did at the 2020 Olympics in Tokyo were a first for her and the sport of gymnastics as a whole. She reached a goal that had been wanted for a long time but never reached: she won Brazil's first-ever Olympic gold medal in gymnastics and a silver medal in the all-around. Not only have these accomplishments raised her profile, but they have also gotten a lot of attention for gymnastics in Brazil, which is usually more interested in football and volleyball. Her wins have changed how people think about gymnastics by showing that it is a sport that takes a lot of skill, discipline, and hard work.

She had a big effect on Brazilian gymnastics in particular. When compared to other sports in Brazil, gymnastics wasn't well-known or funded before Rebeca became famous. Her accomplishments have caused a change in this relationship, giving the sport more attention and respect. Because of all the new attention, young players are much more interested in gymnastics, and more of them are joining clubs and programs across Brazil. The excitement caused by Rebeca's success has helped make sports culture more open and diverse. As a result, gymnastics has gained more attention and support.

Rebecca's impact goes all the way to other countries. Her routines have raised the bar for the sport by combining technical skill with artistic expression in a way that judges and fans all over the world have loved. Her new routines and ways of doing them have affected the development of gymnastics techniques and choreography and inspired other gymnasts. Rebeca's success has shown that ability, hard work, and creativity can all come together to make a gymnast great. This sets a standard for future competitors.

In addition to her sports achievements, Rebeca has shown others how to be strong and not give up. Her ability to come back from injuries and setbacks, especially her recovery from a serious knee injury before the 2020 Olympics, shows how determined and mentally tough you need to be to do well at the top levels of sports. Many young players look up to her and see her as an example of how to deal with problems and still achieve great things.

Rebeca also left behind a legacy of service to the gymnastics community as a whole. Because of her success, more money has been put into the sport, which has led to better facilities, teaching, and support systems for gymnasts. This funding is very important for the future of gymnastics because it will give future athletes the tools they need to do well.

Rebeca's public image and work as an advocate have also made her effect bigger. She has used her fame to help youth development and promote sports education by working with the community and doing good deeds. Being involved in these areas shows that she wants to make a difference in the world beyond her athletic success.

To sum up, Rebeca Andrade's legacy in gymnastics is marked by the groundbreaking things she did, how she changed Brazilian and worldwide gymnastics, and how she became a symbol of strength and excellence. Her work has changed gymnastics forever, inspiring a new breed of athletes and bringing about good changes in the sport. Rebeca has made an indelible mark on the world of gymnastics through her performances, public speaking, and lobbying. Her effect will be felt for years to come.

Conclusion

The story of Rebeca Andrade's rise from a young gymnast in São Paulo to an Olympic champion is an amazing one of skill, determination, and effect. Her gymnastics skills have not only made her one of the best in the sport, but they have also changed the way gymnastics is done in Brazil and around the world.

Her historic wins at the 2020 Tokyo Olympics, which included Brazil's first gold medal in gymnastics and a silver medal in the all-around, have made her famous all over the world. These achievements have not only shown how skilled and dedicated she is, but they have also brought gymnastics in Brazil a level of attention that has never been seen before. Rebeca's success has motivated a new generation of gymnasts and changed how people think about the sport by showing how important and useful it can be as a competitive activity.

Rebecca's influence goes beyond her sports success. Her ability to come back from injuries, her role as a role model, and her gifts to gymnastics as a whole show how committed she is to doing her best and inspiring others. People who are young athletes can relate to her story of strength and drive. It shows what can be done with hard work and persistence.

More money and support have also been put into gymnastics because of Rebeca's impact. This has made the sport more welcoming and helpful for future athletes. Her work with the public and with charities shows that she wants to give back and use her fame to bring about good change.

In conclusion, Rebeca Andrade's legacy is made up of the new things she did, how she changed gymnastics, and how she served as an example of strength and inspiration. Her accomplishments in gymnastics will be remembered for a long time. She will continue to shape the sport and motivate athletes for many years to come. Rebeca's story shows how strong desire can be and how far-reaching the effects of being good at sports can be.

Made in the USA
Columbia, SC
07 May 2025